COLD MESSAGE MASTERY

100+ Templates For Jobs, Internships, Freelancing & Sales

CHAPTERS

Introduction
- Setting the Stage: The Power of Cold Messaging
- Your Roadmap to Cold Messaging Success

What is Cold Messaging and why It's Important
- Chapter 1: Understanding Cold Messaging
- Chapter 2: The Art and Science of Effective Cold Messages
- Chapter 3: The Impact of Cold Messaging in Today's Digital World

Cold Messaging Templates For Jobs & Internships
- Chapter 4: Breaking Into the Job Market with Cold Messaging
- Chapter 5-43: [40 Individual Chapters, each featuring a unique cold message template for Jobs & Internships]

Cold Messaging Templates for Freelancers
- Chapter 44: Crafting Your Freelance Identity Through Cold Messaging
- Chapter 45-74: [30 Individual Chapters, each featuring a unique cold message template for Freelancers]

Cold Messaging Templates for Sales Pitches

Conclusion

INTRODUCTION

SETTING THE STAGE: THE POWER OF COLD MESSAGING

Welcome to 'Cold Message Mastery'

In a world where digital communication reigns supreme, the art of cold messaging has emerged as a pivotal skill for professionals across various domains. Whether you are a student stepping into the workforce, a job seeker exploring new horizons, a freelancer seeking clients or a sales professional aiming to expand your network, mastering cold messaging can be your gateway to unexplored opportunities.

Who This Book Is For

This book is crafted for ambitious individuals like you – eager to make their mark, willing to reach out, and ready to leap into new ventures and professional relationships. If you've ever hesitated to send a message to a potential employer, client, or business partner, fearing it might go unanswered, this book is your ally. Here, you'll find not just templates but strategies, tips, and insights to transform your cold messages into keys that unlock doors of opportunities.

Understanding Cold Messaging

At its core, cold messaging is about initiating conversations without prior interaction. It's the digital equivalent of walking up to someone at a networking event and striking up a conversation. However, in the digital world, your words are your first impression. This book will guide you in crafting messages that not only capture attention but also kindle interest and build connections.

The Importance of Cold Messaging

In today's fast-paced, interconnected world, cold messaging stands as a powerful tool. It breaks barriers, transcends geographies, and offers you a chance to connect with people who can change the course of your career. From securing a dream job, landing a pivotal freelance project, to closing a significant sale, the right message can make all the difference.

Navigating Through the Book

As we journey through this book, we will explore over 100 templates tailored for different scenarios in jobs, internships, freelancing, and sales. Each template is more than just a script; it's a learning tool, designed to provide insights into the nuances of effective communication.

A Word of Encouragement

Embarking on this journey of cold messaging can be both exciting and daunting. Remember, every successful professional you know has, at some point, reached out to someone with a cold message. This book is your companion in this journey, equipping you with the tools, confidence, and skills to open doors to endless possibilities.

Welcome to 'Cold Message Mastery', where your journey to mastering the art of cold messaging begins.

EMBRACING THE ART OF COLD MESSAGING

Discovering the Essence of Cold Communication

In the realm of professional networking and opportunity seeking, cold messaging emerges as a subtle yet powerful tool. It's an art – the art of initiating conversations without a prior connection, akin to a digital handshake extended across cyberspace. In this chapter, we'll uncover the essence of cold messaging and why it's more than just sending out a random message.

Cold Messaging in the Digital Age

With the rise of LinkedIn, email, and other digital platforms, the dynamics of professional communication have evolved. Cold messaging is no longer about sending generic, impersonal emails. It's about crafting a narrative, personalizing your approach, and establishing a connection that resonates with the recipient. We'll explore how digital platforms have transformed cold messaging into a strategic communication tool.

Why Cold Messaging?

Why resort to cold messaging when there are numerous other ways to communicate? This chapter answers this pivotal question. Cold messaging allows you to reach out directly to decision-makers, bypassing traditional gatekeepers. It's about taking the initiative, showcasing your enthusiasm, and demonstrating your value proposition upfront.

The Power of a Well-Crafted Message

A well-crafted cold message can open doors that would otherwise remain closed. It's not just about what you say, but how you say it. This chapter will highlight the components of an effective cold message and how it can make a lasting impression, paving the way for meaningful professional relationships.

Overcoming the Fear of Rejection

One of the biggest hurdles in cold messaging is the fear of being ignored or rejected. Here, we'll discuss how to overcome this fear by understanding the nature of cold messaging and embracing it as a numbers game. We'll also talk about developing resilience and learning from each interaction, regardless of the outcome.

Setting the Stage for Success

As we conclude this chapter, we'll set the stage for the practical journey ahead. Understanding the theoretical underpinnings of cold messaging will empower you to utilize the templates and strategies in the subsequent chapters more effectively.

WHAT IS COLD MESSAGING & WHY IT'S IMPORTANT?

CHAPTER 1: UNDERSTANDING COLD MESSAGING

The Essence of Cold Messaging

At its core, cold messaging is about reaching out to someone you don't know with the hope of establishing a professional connection. It's a proactive approach, where you take the initiative to make contact, often without any prior introduction or mutual connection. This chapter will demystify cold messaging, helping you understand its fundamentals and how it can be a powerful tool in your professional arsenal.

Cold Messaging: Beyond the Basics

Unlike casual or warm networking, where you have a pre-existing connection, cold messaging involves crafting a message to someone you have never interacted with. This could be a potential employer, a client, a mentor, or a leader in your field. The goal is to introduce yourself in a way that prompts a positive response and begins a professional dialogue.

Why Cold Messaging Works

- **Direct Access:** Cold messaging provides a direct line to the people you want to reach, bypassing gatekeepers like secretaries or automated systems.
- **Expanding Networks:** It allows you to expand your professional network beyond your immediate circle, offering opportunities to connect with influencers and decision-makers in your industry.
- **Creating Opportunities:** Cold messaging can open doors to job opportunities, freelance gigs, mentorship, collaborations, and more.

Crafting Your Message

The art of cold messaging lies in how you craft your message. It's not just about what you say, but how you say it. Your message needs to be concise, clear, and compelling. It should convey who you are, what you want, and why the recipient should care. This chapter will lay the foundation for crafting messages that stand out and get responses.

Understanding the Recipient's Perspective

It's crucial to understand the recipient's perspective. They are likely busy and receive numerous messages daily. Your message should respect their time and quickly offer value. This means doing your homework, personalizing your message, and making it clear why you're reaching out to them specifically.

The Power of a Good First Impression

First impressions are vital in cold messaging. Your message is your introduction and sets the tone for any future interaction. A well-crafted message can lead to a positive impression, while a poorly constructed one might get ignored. We'll discuss how to make a good first impression with your cold message.

Conclusion

As we wrap up this chapter, remember that understanding cold messaging is the first step in mastering it. With the foundations laid out here, you're on your way to becoming proficient in this crucial skill. Stay tuned for the next chapter, where we delve into the art and science of crafting effective cold messages.

CHAPTER 2: THE ART AND SCIENCE OF EFFECTIVE COLD MESSAGES

The Intricate Dance of Words and Psychology

Cold messaging, at its heart, is a unique blend of psychological insight and the art of communication. It's about understanding the human psyche and crafting your message to resonate on a personal level. This chapter will take you through this intricate dance, guiding you on how to create messages that not only capture attention but also compel action.

Human Psychology: The Foundation of Response-Driven Messages

- **First Impressions in the Digital World:** Our brains are wired to form first impressions rapidly. In the digital realm, your first message is often your only chance to make a good impression. A successful cold message must be engaging from the first line, drawing the recipient in and making them want to read more.

- **Leveraging Cognitive Biases:** People are naturally drawn to those who share similar interests or backgrounds. Tailoring your message to reflect a shared connection, even if it's a minor one, can significantly increase the likelihood of a response.

- **The Power of Reciprocity:** When you offer something of value, even if it's just a thoughtful insight or a shared interest, you invoke the principle of reciprocity. This psychological principle suggests that people feel compelled to give back when they receive something.

Crafting the Message: The Art of Personalization and Storytelling

- **Beyond Generic Greetings:** Start your message with something that shows you've done your homework. Mention a specific article they wrote, a project they worked on, or a mutual interest. This level of personalization shows genuine interest and sets you apart from generic messages.

- **Storytelling in Brief:** Everyone loves a good story, and a brief, compelling narrative can be a powerful tool in your message. Share a quick story about why you're reaching out to them specifically, making it relevant and engaging.

- **Clarity and Conciseness:** Your message should be clear and to the point. Respect the recipient's time by being concise. Every sentence should add value and move the conversation forward.

The Structure of Your Cold Message

- **The Engaging Opening:** Begin with a hook – something that immediately piques the recipient's interest. It could be a shared connection, an intriguing question, or a compelling statement about their work.
- **The Informative Body:** Here, concisely present your value proposition. What do you bring to the table? Why should they care? Make it about them, not just about what you want.
- **The Compelling Close:** End with a clear, easy-to-respond-to call-to-action. Whether it's a request for a meeting, a phone call, or just a reply, make it simple and straightforward.

Navigating Common Pitfalls

- **Generic Content:** Avoid sending messages that feel like they could have been sent to anyone. Personalization is key.
- **Overwhelming the Recipient:** Don't ask for too much in the first message. Aim to start a conversation, not close a deal.
- **Insufficient Research:** Failing to research your recipient can lead to irrelevant or inappropriate messages. Spend time understanding their background and interests.

Conclusion: The Symphony of Effective Cold Messaging

As this chapter closes, reflect on how combining the scientific understanding of human behavior with the art of personalized communication can elevate your cold messaging. Each message is an opportunity to connect, to impress, and to open doors to new possibilities.

CHAPTER 3: THE IMPACT OF COLD MESSAGING IN TODAY'S DIGITAL WORLD

The Digital Transformation of Professional Communication

The digital era has revolutionized how we connect and communicate, particularly in the professional world. Cold messaging has evolved from an optional skill to a necessary tool in the arsenal of ambitious professionals. This chapter explores the profound impact cold messaging has in our increasingly connected, digital-first world.

Cold Messaging: A Key to Unlocking Digital Doors

- **Breaking Down Geographical Barriers:** Digital platforms have dissolved geographical limitations, allowing professionals to connect with peers, mentors, and potential clients worldwide. Cold messaging is the key that unlocks these global doors.

- **Leveling the Professional Playing Field:** For job seekers, freelancers, and sales professionals, cold messaging offers a direct line to opportunities that were once out of reach. It democratizes access to networks and opportunities, allowing talent and initiative to shine.

The Role of Cold Messaging in Modern Networking

- **Expanding Professional Networks:** Cold messaging enables you to grow your network exponentially, connecting with individuals who can provide new insights, opportunities, and collaborations.
- **Building Personal Brands:** It allows professionals to showcase their expertise, build their personal brand, and position themselves as thought leaders in their field.

Bridging Global Gaps

Cold messaging in the digital world transcends geographical boundaries, bringing a global network within reach. For instance, a freelancer in Hyderabad can now effortlessly connect with a client in New York. This global reach has opened up a plethora of opportunities, making the professional world more accessible and interconnected than ever.

Data That Speaks Volumes

Recent studies have shown that professionals who actively engage in cold messaging are more likely to expand their networks, find new job opportunities, and secure collaborations. For instance, a survey conducted in 2023 revealed that 60% of freelancers who used targeted cold messaging strategies experienced a significant increase in client engagement.

Navigating Digital Communication Norms

Understanding the nuances of digital communication is vital. For example, LinkedIn messages should be professional and concise, reflecting the platform's business-centric nature. In contrast, Twitter allows for more casual and succinct outreach. Respecting these platform-specific nuances can significantly enhance the effectiveness of your cold messaging efforts.

Cold Messaging: A Look into the Future

As we look to the future, emerging trends like AI-driven personalization and increased emphasis on multimedia content in messages will shape the landscape of cold messaging. Staying abreast of these trends and adapting your strategies accordingly will be key to maintaining the effectiveness of your cold messaging endeavors.

Embracing the Digital Shift for Professional

Success

In conclusion, the digital world has not only enhanced the importance of cold messaging but also expanded its potential. By embracing this shift and leveraging the power of cold messaging, professionals can unlock doors to global opportunities and unprecedented professional growth.

COLD MESSAGING TEMPLATES FOR JOBS & INTERNSHIPS

CHAPTER 4: BREAKING INTO THE JOB MARKET WITH COLD MESSAGING

Introduction

The job market today is a maze of opportunities and challenges. In this competitive landscape, cold messaging emerges as a beacon of hope for job seekers and internship aspirants. It's a proactive approach to unlock doors to potential opportunities. This chapter guides you through the process of using cold messaging effectively to navigate and stand out in the job market.

Identifying Your Targets

The first crucial step in your cold messaging journey is identifying the right targets. This involves:

- Researching companies that align with your career goals.
- Identifying key individuals in those organizations, such as hiring managers, department heads, or potential team leads.
- Understanding the company culture and values to tailor your message accordingly.

Crafting a Narrative That Resonates

Your cold message should not be a mere introduction but a narrative that resonates with the recipient:

- Start with why you are interested in the company or the specific role.
- Include a brief but powerful introduction of yourself, focusing on skills and experiences that are most relevant to the target role or organization.
- Make a connection between your career aspirations and the company's goals or recent achievements.

Subject Line: Your First Impression

In email-based cold messaging, the subject line is your first impression:

- Craft subject lines that are concise, clear, and compelling. For example, "Aspiring Marketing Specialist Inspired by Your Recent Campaign" or "Recent Graduate Eager to Contribute to Your IT

Team."

- Personalize where possible. Mentioning the recipient's name or a recent company event can make your email stand out.

The Opening: Establishing a Connection

The opening lines of your message are crucial in establishing a connection:

- If you have a referral, mention it upfront. For example, "John Doe, your colleague from the sales department, suggested I reach out to you..."
- If you don't have a referral, find common ground or express genuine admiration for a recent company achievement or the recipient's work.

Articulating Your Value Proposition

This is where you present what you can offer:

- Highlight your skills and experiences that are most relevant to the company or the role you are interested in.
- Be specific about your achievements. Instead of saying, "I have great marketing skills," say, "I led a marketing campaign that increased social media engagement by 30%."

Making the Ask

Be clear about what you are asking for:

- Whether it's an informational interview, guidance, or consideration for a role, your request should be straightforward and respectful.
- End with a call to action, like, "I would appreciate the opportunity to discuss how my skills in digital marketing could benefit your team."

Real-Life Example: A Success Story

Consider the story of Priya, who used a well-crafted LinkedIn message to land an interview at her dream company. She started with a strong subject line, expressed her admiration for the company's innovative approach to technology, and clearly articulated how her background in software engineering and her project experience made her a great fit for the role.

Conclusion

Cold messaging, when done right, can be a powerful tool in your job-seeking arsenal. It's about making that first impression count and opening up a dialogue. As you proceed with your job search, remember that each cold message is a step towards your dream job.

CHAPTER 5-43: COLD MESSAGING TEMPLATES FOR JOBS & INTERNSHIPS

Template 1: Reaching Out to a Hiring Manager

Subject: Inspired by [Company's] Innovation – Aspiring Product Manager

Dear [Hiring Manager's Name],

I recently came across [Company's] groundbreaking work in [specific project or product]. As an aspiring product manager with a passion for innovation and a strong background in [relevant experience or skill], I am keenly interested in contributing to such a dynamic team. I believe my experience in [specific relevant experience] aligns well with the vision of [Company]. Could we schedule a brief call to discuss potential opportunities in your team?

Best regards,
[Your Name]

Template 2: Connecting with a Potential Mentor for an Internship

Subject: Seeking Guidance and Insight in [Industry/Field]

Hi [Potential Mentor's Name],

I am [Your Name], a [Your Year] student at [Your University] majoring in [Your Major]. Your work in [specific aspect of the industry/field] has been a major source of inspiration for me. I am currently seeking an internship that allows me to deepen my understanding and skills in [specific area]. I would be grateful for the opportunity to learn from someone as experienced as you. Could we connect over a coffee or a quick call for some advice and guidance?

Warm regards,
[Your Name]

Template 3: Cold Email to a Company with No Advertised Openings

Subject: Proactive Inquiry – Opportunities in [Company's Department/Field]

Dear [Recipient's Name],

I am writing to inquire about potential opportunities in [Company's Department/Field]. My background in [relevant experience or education] and my passion for [specific aspect related to the company's work] make me keen to explore how I could contribute to your team. While I understand there may not be current openings, I am interested in any future opportunities. May I send over my resume for consideration in upcoming roles?

Thank you for your time,
[Your Name]

Template 4: Responding to a Job Posting

Subject: Application for [Job Title] – [Your Name]

Dear [Recipient's Name],

I am writing to express my interest in the recently advertised [Job Title] position. With a [degree or certification] in [relevant field] and [number of years] years of experience in [specific experience related to the job], I am excited about the opportunity to contribute to [Company]. My experience in [specific relevant experience or project] has equipped me with [specific skills or knowledge] that I believe aligns well with the needs of your team. I have attached my resume for your review and would welcome the chance to discuss how my background and skills would be a good fit for [Company].

Sincerely,
[Your Name]

Template 5: Networking Email to an Industry Professional

Subject: Admirer of Your Work in [Industry] – [Your Name]

Hello [Professional's Name],

I've been following your work in [Industry or Specific Project] and have been genuinely inspired by your contributions. I am [Your Name], currently working in [Your Current Role/Field] and looking to transition into [Target Industry/Role]. Your insights and experiences would be invaluable to someone at the beginning of this journey like myself. Might you have time for a brief chat to share some advice?

Warm regards,
[Your Name]

Template 6: Inquiry for Internship Opportunities at a Startup

Subject: Eager to Contribute to [Startup's Name] as an Intern

Hi [Recipient's Name],

As a student passionate about [specific field or technology relevant to the startup], I am impressed by [Startup's Name] and its innovative approach to [specific project or product]. I am seeking an internship where I can contribute meaningfully while enhancing my skills. Although I didn't find any open internship positions listed, I am keen to explore any potential opportunities. Can we discuss how my background in [Your Background/Skills] might align with your team's needs?

Best,
[Your Name]

Template 7: Approaching a Company Representative Met at an Event

Subject: Following Up from [Event Name]

Dear [Representative's Name],

It was a pleasure meeting you at [Event Name]. I enjoyed our conversation about [specific topic discussed]. As I mentioned, I am very interested in the [specific area or role] at [Company's Name]. Based on our discussion, it seems like my experience with [specific experience or skill] could be a good fit. May I follow up with my resume and potentially discuss this further?

Thank you,
[Your Name]

Template 8: Cold Message to a Recent Acquaintance for Job Referral

Subject: Requesting Guidance on a Role at

[Company's Name]

Hi [Acquaintance's Name],

It was great connecting with you at [where you met]. I recall you mentioning that you work at [Company's Name], and I recently came across an opening for [Job Title] which aligns perfectly with my expertise in [your expertise/field]. I'm keen to apply and was wondering if you could offer any insights into the role or the team. If you think it's appropriate, would you be comfortable referring my application?

Thanks a lot for your help,
[Your Name]

Template 9: Reaching Out to a Company After a Layoff Announcement

Subject: Interested in Contributing to [Company's Name] Post-Layoff

Dear [Recipient's Name],

I recently read about the layoffs at [Company's Name] and wanted to reach out. Having experienced a similar situation, I understand the challenges it brings. I'm currently seeking opportunities where my skills in [your skills/field] can be put to good use. I admire [Company's Name] for its [something positive about the company], and I believe my experience with [specific experience or project] could be beneficial during this transition period. Could we discuss potential opportunities for collaboration or roles where I might contribute?

Best regards,
[Your Name]

Template 10: Cold Email to an Alumni for Job Referral

Subject: [Your University] Alumnus Seeking Insight at [Company's Name]

Hello [Alumni's Name],

As a fellow [Your University] alumnus, I've been keenly following your career journey and am impressed by your accomplishments at [Company's Name]. I'm currently exploring opportunities in [specific field or department] and am very interested in [Company's Name]. Your insights would be invaluable to me as I navigate this process. Could I ask for your advice on applying, and if appropriate, a referral for the open [Job Title] role?

Warm regards,
[Your Name]

Template 11: Message to a Company Leader About a Job Interest

Subject: Inspired by Your Leadership at [Company's Name] – [Your Name]

Dear [Leader's Name],

Your recent talk on [specific topic] resonated deeply

with me, especially your insights on [specific point]. I'm [Your Name], with a background in [your background] and a strong interest in [specific area related to the company]. I believe my skills and experiences could contribute significantly to [Company's Name], particularly in [specific area or project you're interested in]. Could we discuss potential opportunities within your team?

Sincerely,
[Your Name]

Template 12: Inquiring About Internship Opportunities in a Niche Field

Subject: Aspiring [Your Field] Intern Intrigued by [Company's Name] Work

Hi [Recipient's Name],

I'm a [Your Year] student at [Your University], majoring in [Your Major], with a strong interest in [specific niche field]. I've been following [Company's Name] and am particularly intrigued by your work in [specific project or area]. I am eager to gain hands-on experience in this niche. Though I haven't found specific internship listings in this area, I am curious to know if [Company's Name] might consider an intern in this capacity. I'd be thrilled to contribute and learn.

Thank you for considering,
[Your Name]

Template 13: Reaching Out for a Research Position

Subject: Keen Interest in [Research Topic] at [Company or Institution's Name]

Dear [Recipient's Name],

I am deeply fascinated by the research on [Research Topic] conducted at [Company or Institution's Name]. As a recent graduate with a degree in [Your Degree] and hands-on experience in [Related Experience], I am eager to contribute to and learn from such a pioneering environment. I have worked on [Brief Description of a Related Project or Paper], which aligns closely with your work. Could we discuss potential research positions or opportunities for collaboration?

Best,
[Your Name]

Template 14: Cold Message to a Potential Internship Supervisor

Subject: Aspiring Intern Interested in [Specific Internship Area]

Hello [Supervisor's Name],

I came across your profile while researching [Specific Internship Area] opportunities at [Company's Name]. Your role in [Specific Project or Aspect of Work] particularly caught my attention. I am currently a student at [Your University], majoring in [Your Major], and am very interested in an internship under your supervision. My experience with [Specific Skill or Project] has equipped me with a strong foundation in [Relevant Field or Skill]. Could we discuss the possibility of me joining your team as an intern?

Thank you for your time,
[Your Name]

Template 15: Email to a Company for a Junior Role

Subject: Enthusiastic Applicant for the Junior [Role] Position

Dear [Hiring Manager's Name],

I recently discovered the Junior [Role] opening at [Company's Name] and am excited about the opportunity to apply. With a [Degree or Certification] in [Relevant Field] and a passion for [Relevant Skills or Area of Work], I am eager to start my professional journey in an innovative and challenging environment like yours. During my time at [University or Previous Job], I gained valuable experience in [Specific Experience or Project], which I believe would be beneficial in this role. I have attached my resume and would be honored to discuss how my background aligns with [Company's Name]'s needs.

Sincerely,
[Your Name]

Template 16: LinkedIn Message to a Recruiter

Subject: Interest in [Role/Department] Opportunities at [Company's Name]

Hi [Recruiter's Name],

I recently came across your profile on LinkedIn and noticed that you recruit for [Company's Name]'s [Role/Department]. I am highly interested in exploring career opportunities in this field, given my background in [Relevant Background] and my experience with [Specific Skills or Projects]. I believe that my expertise could contribute significantly to [Company's Name]. Could we connect to discuss current or future opportunities that might align with my profile?

Best regards,
[Your Name]

Template 17: Cold Email to a Company for a Career Change

Subject: Transitioning to [New Field] – Exploring Opportunities at [Company's Name]

Dear [Recipient's Name],

I am currently in the process of transitioning my career towards [New Field] and am very interested in opportunities at [Company's Name]. Although my background has primarily been in [Previous Field], the skills and experiences I have gained are highly transferable and relevant. For instance, my experience in [Specific Aspect of Previous Field] complements the requirements of [New Field]. I am particularly drawn to [Company's Name] because of [Specific Reason or Company's Project]. Could we discuss how my unique background might fit within your team?

Warm regards,
[Your Name]

Template 18: Inquiring About Internship Opportunities in a Creative Field

Subject: Passionate about [Creative Field] – Seeking Internship Opportunities at [Company's Name]

Hi [Recipient's Name],

I am an avid admirer of the creative work produced by [Company's Name], particularly in [specific project or area]. As a [Your Current Status, e.g., 'final-year student at XYZ University majoring in ABC'], I am seeking an internship that allows me to delve deeper into [Creative Field]. I have honed my skills through [mention any relevant project or experience], and I am enthusiastic about the possibility of contributing to your team. Are there any internship opportunities available where I could bring my creative energy and learn from the best?

Kind regards,
[Your Name]

Template 19: Cold Email to a Tech Company for a Software Development Role

Subject: Enthusiastic Developer Interested in [Specific Technology or Project] at [Company's Name]

Dear [Recipient's Name],

I recently came across [Company's Name]'s innovative project in [Specific Technology or Project], and it resonated strongly with my professional interests and skills. With a background in software development, particularly in [specific languages or technologies], I believe I could be a valuable addition to your team. I have experience with [mention a specific project or accomplishment], which aligns well with your current projects. I would appreciate the opportunity to discuss how my technical skills and passion for technology can contribute to the groundbreaking work at [Company's Name].

Best,
[Your Name]

Template 20: Reaching Out to a Non-Profit Organization for Volunteer Opportunities

Subject: Eager to Contribute to [Non-Profit Organization's Name]'s Mission

Hello [Recipient's Name],

I have been deeply inspired by the mission and work of [Non-Profit Organization's Name], especially your recent initiatives in [specific area or project]. I am keen to offer my skills and time as a volunteer. My background in [Your Background/Skills] aligns with your organization's goals, and I am particularly interested in contributing to [specific project or area]. Could you guide me on how to get involved and make a meaningful impact through your organization?

Thank you for your consideration,
[Your Name]

Template 21: Cold Messaging a Potential Collaborator in Research

Subject: Exploring Collaborative Research Opportunities in [Research Area]

Dear [Researcher's Name],

I am [Your Name], a researcher specializing in [Your Research Area]. I recently read your paper on [Specific Aspect of Their Research], and it closely aligns with my current work on [Your Research Topic]. I believe that a collaboration between us could lead to significant advancements in this field. Would you be open to discussing potential collaborative research opportunities, perhaps in the form of a joint study or paper?

Sincerely,

[Your Name]

Template 22: Approaching a Company for a Career Fair or Workshop Participation

Subject: Invitation to Participate in [Your University/Institution's Name] Career Fair

Dear [Company Representative's Name],

I am [Your Name], representing the career services department at [Your University/Institution's Name]. We are hosting a career fair on [Date], and it would be an honor to have [Company's Name] participate. Our students are particularly interested in [specific fields or areas relevant to the company], and your presence would provide invaluable insight and opportunities. Could we discuss the possibility of your participation and how we could facilitate a mutually beneficial experience?

Looking forward to your response,
[Your Name]

Template 23: Contacting a Company for a Remote Work Opportunity

Subject: Seeking Remote Work Opportunities in [Field/Area] at [Company's Name]

Hello [Recipient's Name],

I am deeply impressed by the work culture and innovative projects at [Company's Name], particularly your commitment to flexible work environments. As a professional with extensive experience in [Your Field/Area], I am seeking opportunities to contribute remotely. My background includes [mention specific skills or experiences relevant to remote work and the company's field]. Could we explore potential remote roles where my expertise aligns with your team's needs?

Warm regards,
[Your Name]

Template 24: Cold Email to a Start-Up Founder for a Potential Role

Subject: Enthusiastic to Contribute to [Start-Up's Name]'s Growth in [Field/Area]

Dear [Founder's Name],

I have been following [Start-Up's Name] since its inception and am truly inspired by its vision and impact in [Field/Area]. As someone passionate about [relevant interest or skill], I am eager to contribute to a team that is making waves in the industry. My experience in [mention relevant experience or projects] has equipped me with the skills necessary to thrive in a start-up environment. I would love the opportunity to discuss how I can contribute to your team's success.

Sincerely,
[Your Name]

Template 25: Reaching Out for a Part-Time Position or Internship

Subject: Interested in Part-Time [Position/Role] Opportunities at [Company's Name]

Hi [Recipient's Name],

I am currently a [Your Current Status, e.g., 'student' or 'freelancer'] looking for part-time opportunities in [Field/Area]. I came across [Company's Name] and was impressed by [specific aspect of the company]. My background in [relevant skills or experience] seems well-suited for [Company's Name]'s needs. I'm particularly interested in [mention any specific project or department if applicable]. Are there any part-time roles or internships available where I could bring value and gain invaluable experience?

Best,
[Your Name]

Template 26: Messaging a Professional for a Job Shadowing Opportunity

Subject: Requesting Job Shadowing Opportunity in [Field/Area] at [Company's Name]

Dear [Professional's Name],

I am [Your Name], currently exploring career paths in [Field/Area]. I have great admiration for your work at [Company's Name], and I believe that observing a professional like you in action would provide me with invaluable insights. Would you be open to allowing me to shadow you for a day or two? I am keen to learn and would ensure that my presence is as non-intrusive as possible.

Thank you for considering,
[Your Name]

Template 27: Cold Email to a Human Resources Manager for Career Opportunities

Subject: Exploring Career Opportunities in [Field/Area] at [Company's Name]

Dear [HR Manager's Name],

I am reaching out to inquire about career opportunities in [Field/Area] at [Company's Name]. With a [degree or certification] in [relevant field] and experience in [specific experience or skills], I am keen to join a company that values [mention any specific company values or projects that resonate with you]. My experience in [specific relevant experience] aligns with the innovative work being done at [Company's Name]. Could you guide me on current or upcoming openings that might fit my profile?

Looking forward to your guidance,
[Your Name]

Template 28: Inquiry for a Graduate Program Position

Subject: Interested in the [Graduate Program Name] at [Company's Name]

Hi [Recipient's Name],

I am [Your Name], a recent graduate from [Your University] with a degree in [Your Degree]. I am very interested in the [Graduate Program Name] at [Company's Name]. My academic background and internships in [relevant field or experience] have prepared me well for the challenges and learning opportunities your program offers. I am particularly drawn to [Company's Name] because of [specific reason or project]. Could you provide some insights into the application process or any advice for a prospective applicant like me?

Kind regards,
[Your Name]

Template 29: Cold Email to a Hiring Manager for a Career Transition

Subject: Transitioning to [New Career Field] – Interested in Opportunities at [Company's Name]

Dear [Hiring Manager's Name],

As a professional looking to transition into [New Career Field], I am writing to explore potential opportunities at [Company's Name]. While my previous experience has been in [Previous Career Field], the skills I have developed are highly relevant and transferrable. For instance, [mention a specific skill or experience that applies to the new field]. I am particularly interested in [Company's Name] due to [specific reason, project, or company value]. May I send my resume for your review for any suitable positions?

Thank you for your time,
[Your Name]

Template 30: Reaching Out for a Speculative Application

Subject: Speculative Application – Interested in [Field/Area] Roles at [Company's Name]

Hello [Recipient's Name],

I am writing to express my interest in potential opportunities in the field of [Field/Area] at [Company's Name]. Although I did not find specific openings that match my profile, I am keen to offer my skills and expertise to your team. My experience in [mention relevant experience or projects] aligns well with the innovative approach of [Company's Name]. I would appreciate the chance to discuss how I could contribute to your ongoing and future projects.

Best regards,
[Your Name]

Template 31: LinkedIn Message to a Company Executive

Subject: Inspired by Your Vision – Seeking Guidance at [Company's Name]

Dear [Executive's Name],

I recently heard your talk on [specific topic or vision] and was truly inspired by your perspective and the direction [Company's Name] is heading. I am [Your Name], with a background in [Your Background], and I am interested in exploring career opportunities at your company. Your guidance or any insights on joining a team that shares such a forward-thinking approach would be invaluable. May I ask for a few minutes of your time for a brief conversation?

Sincerely,
[Your Name]

Template 32: Cold Email to a Small Business for a Potential Role

Subject: Enthusiastic About Contributing to [Small Business's Name]

Hi [Business Owner's Name],

I came across [Small Business's Name] and was impressed with your work in [specific area or project]. As a [Your Profession] with experience in [Your Experience/Skills], I am eager to contribute to a growing business like yours. I believe my background in [specific relevant experience] can help [specific goal or project of the business]. Are there any roles or projects within your team where my skills could be a good fit?

Looking forward to the possibility of working together,
[Your Name]

Template 33: Approaching a Company for a Specific Project Interest

Subject: Enthusiastic about [Specific Project] at [Company's Name]

Hi [Recipient's Name],

I recently came across [Specific Project] at [Company's Name], and it perfectly aligns with my professional interests and skills. I am [Your Name], a [Your Professional Title] with extensive experience in [Your Area of Expertise]. I am particularly impressed by [something specific about the project] and would love the opportunity to contribute to its success. Are there any roles available on this project where my expertise in [Your Specific Skills] would be beneficial?

Best regards,
[Your Name]

Template 34: Cold Email to a Company for a Recent Graduate Role

Subject: Recent [Your Degree] Graduate Eager to Join

[Company's Name]

Dear [Recipient's Name],

I am a recent graduate from [Your University] with a degree in [Your Degree], and I am very interested in starting my career at [Company's Name]. My academic background, coupled with my internship experience in [relevant experience], has prepared me well for the challenges at [Company's Name]. I am particularly drawn to your company because of [specific reason related to the company's work or culture]. Could you guide me on how to best apply for recent graduate roles in your company?

Thank you for your consideration,
[Your Name]

Template 35: Messaging for a Seasonal or Temporary Position

Subject: Interested in Seasonal Opportunities in [Field/Area] at [Company's Name]

Hello [Recipient's Name],

As the season for [relevant season or event] approaches, I am writing to inquire about any seasonal or temporary positions available at [Company's Name] in [Field/Area]. With my experience in [Your Experience/Skills], I believe I can offer valuable support during this busy period. During my previous role at [Previous Company or Project], I successfully managed [specific task or project relevant to the seasonal job]. I am excited about the possibility of bringing my skills to [Company's Name].

Warm regards,
[Your Name]

Template 36: Reaching Out to a Local Business for Job Opportunities

Subject: Keen to Contribute to [Local Business's Name]

Dear [Business Owner's Name],

I am a local resident passionate about contributing to businesses within our community. I have been a loyal customer of [Local Business's Name] and am impressed with your [specific aspect of the business]. As a [Your Profession] with skills in [Your Skills], I am interested in exploring how I could contribute to your team. Are there any current or upcoming opportunities where my background in [specific experience or skills] might fit your business needs?

Sincerely,
[Your Name]

Template 37: Inquiring About Unadvertised Roles in a Niche Industry

Subject: Exploring Unadvertised Opportunities in [Niche Industry] at [Company's Name]

Hello [Recipient's Name],

I am writing to you with a keen interest in [Niche Industry]. While I am aware that [Company's Name] has not advertised any current openings in this area, I am eager to explore any potential unadvertised opportunities. My experience in [Your Experience] and my passion for [specific aspect of the niche industry] align closely with the work your company is renowned for. I would appreciate any information or guidance on opportunities in this niche area within your company.

Best,
[Your Name]

Template 38: Reaching Out for an International Job Opportunity

Subject: International Career Aspirations – Interested in [Job Title] at [Company's Name] in [Country]

Dear [Recipient's Name],

I am writing from [Your Country] with a strong interest in the [Job Title] position at [Company's Name] in [Country]. My professional experience in [Your Field/Industry] and my familiarity with [specific skills or aspects relevant to the job and country] make me a suitable candidate for this role. Having followed [Company's Name] for some time, I am particularly impressed by [specific project or aspect of the company]. Could we discuss the possibility of international recruitment and how my background could contribute to your team?

Best regards,
[Your Name]

Template 39: Cold Email to a Senior Professional for Career Advice in a New Field

Subject: Seeking Career Advice in [New Field] – [Your Name]

Hello [Professional's Name],

I recently made the decision to transition my career into [New Field]. I have admired your work and career path in this field for some time. As I navigate this transition, your insights and advice would be incredibly valuable. I come from a background in [Your Previous Field], and I believe there are transferable skills that I can bring to [New Field]. Would you be willing to share some guidance or recommendations on how best to approach this career shift?

Warm regards,
[Your Name]

Template 40: Messaging a Company Representative After a Job Fair

Subject: Following Up from [Job Fair Name]

Hi [Representative's Name],

It was a pleasure meeting you at [Job Fair Name]. I enjoyed our conversation about the opportunities at [Company's Name], especially in the field of [specific field or department]. As I mentioned during our talk, I am very interested in the [specific role or type of work] at [Company's Name]. I believe my background in [Your Background], particularly my experience in [specific experience or project], aligns well with your team's goals. Could you advise on the best way to formally apply or whom to contact for further steps?

Thank you,
[Your Name]

COLD MESSAGING TEMPLATES FOR FREELANCING

CHAPTER 44: CRAFTING YOUR FREELANCE IDENTITY THROUGH COLD MESSAGING

Introduction

In the world of freelancing, your identity and personal brand are crucial to attracting clients and projects. Cold messaging can be a powerful tool for freelancers to showcase their unique skills and value propositions to potential clients. This chapter guides you on how to craft effective cold messages that resonate with your freelance identity and appeal to potential clients.

Understanding Your Unique Selling Proposition

Before crafting your cold messages, it's vital to understand and articulate your unique selling proposition (USP). This involves:

- Identifying your niche or specialization.
- Highlighting your unique skills or experiences that set you apart.
- Understanding the specific needs and pain points of your target clients.

Tailoring Your Message to Your Target Client

Your cold message should speak directly to the needs and interests of your target client:

- Research your potential client's business, industry, and recent projects to tailor your message.
- Emphasize how your skills and experience can solve their specific challenges or contribute to their projects.

Structuring Your Cold Message

A well-structured cold message for freelancing should include:

- A clear and engaging subject line that piques interest.
- An introduction that briefly states who you are and your area of expertise.
- A body that highlights your USP, relevant experience, and how you can benefit the client.

- A call to action, such as asking for a brief meeting or offering to send a portfolio.

Building a Connection

Beyond selling your services, aim to establish a connection with the potential client:

- Show genuine interest in their work or recent achievements.
- If applicable, mention any mutual connections or shared professional affiliations.

Sample Cold Message Template for a Freelancer

Subject: Elevating Your Brand with Professional Graphic Design

Hi [Client's Name],

I came across your recent campaign for [Client's Company/Product], and I was impressed by your approach to [specific aspect]. As a freelance graphic designer specializing in brand development, I have helped businesses like yours create visually compelling stories. My work with [mention a notable project or client] resulted in [specific positive outcome]. I'd love to discuss how my design expertise can enhance your next campaign. May I send over my portfolio for your review?

Best,
[Your Name]

Conclusion

Crafting a strong freelance identity through cold messaging is about combining your unique skills and experiences with a deep understanding of your potential clients' needs. This chapter sets the foundation for creating messages that not only showcase your abilities but also build meaningful professional relationships.

CHAPTER 45-74: COLD MESSAGING TEMPLATES FOR FREELANCING

Template 1: Graphic Designer Offering Services

Subject: Enhancing Your Brand's Visual Impact – Freelance Graphic Designer Available

Hello [Client's Name],

I am a freelance graphic designer with a knack for creating visually engaging and brand-aligned designs. I've admired [Company's Name]'s approach to branding and believe my style complements your aesthetic well. I recently worked on a project for [Previous Client/Project], which resulted in [specific outcome or achievement]. Would it be possible to discuss how my design expertise could enhance your upcoming projects? I'd be happy to share my portfolio.

Best regards,
[Your Name]

Template 2: Freelance Writer Pitching Content Ideas

Subject: Captivating Content for [Company's Name] – Freelance Writer Proposal

Hi [Client's Name],

I'm a freelance writer specializing in [specific industry or content type], and I've been following your work at [Company's Name]. Your recent piece on [specific topic] resonated with me, and I have some content ideas that could complement your upcoming editorial calendar. My previous work with [mention previous publication or company] was well-received for its [specific aspect]. Could I share a few content ideas that might interest your audience?

Warm regards,
[Your Name]

Template 3: Web Developer Offering Redesign Services

Subject: Transform Your Website with Professional Web Development

Dear [Client's Name],

As an experienced freelance web developer, I

specialize in creating intuitive and responsive websites. I came across [Company's Name]'s website and saw potential for enhancing user experience and design. For instance, my recent project with [Previous Client/Project] involved a complete redesign that led to a [specific improvement, like increased traffic]. I would love to discuss how a website redesign could benefit your company. May I send over some of my work samples and ideas?

Thank you,
[Your Name]

Template 4: Social Media Consultant Reaching Out

Subject: Boosting [Company's Name]'s Social Media Presence

Hi [Client's Name],

I am a freelance social media consultant with a focus on [specific industry or type of social media]. I've been impressed with [Company's Name]'s social media presence, but I see opportunities for even greater engagement and reach. For example, my recent campaign for [Previous Client/Project] resulted in [specific results or growth metrics]. I'd like to share some strategies that could elevate your social media efforts. Can we schedule a time to chat?

Best,
[Your Name]

Template 5: Freelance Photographer Offering

Services for Events

Subject: Capturing Memorable Moments – Freelance Photography for [Company's Name]

Hello [Client's Name],

I am a professional freelance photographer with extensive experience in capturing [specific type of events or subjects]. I noticed that [Company's Name] frequently hosts events and thought my expertise could be of service. My photography at [Previous Event/Project] was praised for [specific aspect, like creativity or capturing emotions]. I'd love to discuss how my photography services could add value to your upcoming events. May I share my portfolio with you?

Sincerely,
[Your Name]

Template 6: Freelance SEO Specialist Offering Services

Subject: Enhance Your Online Presence with Expert SEO Services

Hello [Client's Name],

I am a freelance SEO specialist dedicated to helping businesses increase their online visibility. After reviewing [Company's Name]'s website, I noticed opportunities for SEO optimization that could significantly boost your search engine rankings. I've successfully implemented strategies for [Previous Client/Project] that resulted in [specific improvement, e.g., increased organic traffic]. Can we schedule a call to discuss how I can assist in enhancing your website's SEO?

Kind regards,
[Your Name]

Template 7: Freelance Video Editor Reaching Out

Subject: Elevating [Company's Name]'s Video Content – Freelance Editing Services

Hi [Client's Name],

I'm a freelance video editor with a passion for crafting compelling visual stories. I've been impressed with the video content from [Company's Name] and see great potential for further elevating its impact. My recent work on [specific project or type of content] for [Previous Client] was praised for [specific achievement or quality]. I'd love to discuss how my editing skills could enhance your upcoming video projects. May I share some of my work with you?

Warm regards,
[Your Name]

Template 8: Freelance UI/UX Designer Offering Design Audit

Subject: UI/UX Design Audit Offer for [Company's

Name]

Dear [Client's Name],

As a UI/UX designer specializing in creating user-friendly and aesthetically pleasing digital experiences, I am offering a complimentary design audit for select businesses this month. I've noticed [Company's Name]'s app/website and believe there's potential to enhance user engagement through design improvements. My work with [Previous Client/Project] led to [specific results, like improved user retention]. Would you be interested in a free UI/UX audit for your digital platforms?

Thank you,
[Your Name]

Template 9: Freelance Content Strategist Proposing Services

Subject: Propelling [Company's Name]'s Content Strategy Forward

Hi [Client's Name],

I am a content strategist with a focus on driving engagement and building brand presence. Your content at [Company's Name] aligns closely with my expertise, and I believe there are opportunities to further amplify its reach and impact. For instance, my content strategy for [Previous Client] resulted in [specific outcome, like increased engagement]. I'd like to explore how my strategic approach to content could align with your goals. Can we set up a time to discuss this?

Best,
[Your Name]

Template 10: Freelance Digital Marketer for E-commerce Business

Subject: Boosting [Company's Name]'s E-commerce Performance

Hello [Client's Name],

As a digital marketer specializing in e-commerce, I've developed strategies that significantly boost online sales and customer engagement. I'm particularly impressed with [Company's Name]'s online store but noticed some areas for potential growth. For example, my campaign for [Previous Client/Project] enhanced online sales by [specific percentage]. I'd love to share how a tailored digital marketing strategy could achieve similar results for your store. Would you be open to discussing this?

Sincerely,
[Your Name]

Template 11: Freelance Virtual Assistant Offering Services

Subject: Streamline Your Workflow – Freelance Virtual Assistant Services Available

Hi [Client's Name],

I am a skilled freelance virtual assistant, and I specialize in supporting busy professionals and entrepreneurs with [list specific services, e.g., administrative tasks, scheduling, email management]. After learning about [Company's Name] and your role as [Client's Position], I believe my services could help streamline your workflow and increase productivity. I've successfully assisted clients like [Previous Client/Project], leading to [specific outcome, e.g., more organized operations]. Can we discuss how my services could meet your needs?

Best regards,
[Your Name]

Template 12: Freelance Illustrator Reaching Out to Publishing Houses

Subject: Bringing Stories to Life – Freelance Illustration Services

Hello [Client's Name],

I'm a freelance illustrator with a passion for creating engaging and evocative book illustrations. Your recent publications at [Publishing House's Name] have captured my attention, and I feel my artistic style would be a perfect fit. My previous work on [Previous Project or Book Title] was well-received for its [specific style or feedback]. I'd love to discuss potential collaboration on upcoming projects. May I share my portfolio with you?

Warm regards,
[Your Name]

Template 13: Freelance Data Analyst Offering Data Insights

Subject: Enhance Your Data-Driven Decisions – Freelance Data Analyst

Dear [Client's Name],

As a freelance data analyst, I specialize in turning data into actionable insights. I noticed that [Company's Name] is growing rapidly in [specific sector or field], and I believe my analytical skills could provide valuable insights to inform your strategic decisions. My recent project with [Previous Client] resulted in [specific improvement or discovery]. I'd appreciate the opportunity to discuss how my data analysis services could benefit your team.

Thank you,
[Your Name]

Template 14: Freelance Copywriter Pitching to E-commerce Brands

Subject: Elevating Product Descriptions – Freelance Copywriting for [Company's Name]

Hi [Client's Name],

I am a freelance copywriter with a focus on

crafting compelling product descriptions that drive sales and enhance brand voice. I've been impressed with [Company's Name]'s e-commerce platform but noticed some areas where an enhanced copy could further boost customer engagement. For instance, my work for [Previous Client/Product Line] led to an increase in conversion rates by [specific percentage]. I'd be thrilled to share how effective copywriting could enhance your product listings. Can we schedule a chat to discuss this?

Best,
[Your Name]

Template 15: Freelance Business Consultant Offering Strategy Services

Subject: Strategic Growth Opportunities for [Company's Name]

Hello [Client's Name],

As a business consultant specializing in [specific area, e.g., growth strategies, operational efficiency], I offer expertise that can propel businesses to their next growth phase. Your work at [Company's Name] in [specific field or project] is impressive, and I see the potential for even greater success. In my recent consultancy with [Previous Client], we achieved [specific results or improvements]. I would welcome a discussion on how my strategic approach could align with your business goals.

Sincerely,

[Your Name]

Template 16: Freelance Social Media Manager Offering Services

Subject: Maximizing [Company's Name]'s Social Media Impact

Hi [Client's Name],

I'm a freelance social media manager with a track record of elevating online presence and engagement. I've been following [Company's Name] and believe there's great potential to enhance your social media strategy. My recent work for [Previous Client] resulted in [specific achievements, like increased follower count or engagement rate]. I'd love to discuss how a tailored social media plan could amplify your brand's reach. May I share some ideas with you?

Best regards,
[Your Name]

Template 17: Freelance Event Planner Reaching Out to Corporates

Subject: Elevate Your Corporate Events – Expert Freelance Planning Services

Dear [Client's Name],

As a seasoned freelance event planner specializing in corporate events, I have a keen eye for creating memorable and impactful experiences. I understand that [Company's Name] frequently hosts [type of events, e.g., conferences, workshops], and I believe my expertise could significantly enhance these events. My work with [Previous Client or Event] was praised for [specific success or feature]. Can we discuss how my services could add value to your upcoming events?

Warm regards,
[Your Name]

Template 18: Freelance Public Relations Specialist Offering Campaign Ideas

Subject: Boosting [Company's Name]'s Public Image and Brand Awareness

Hi [Client's Name],

I am a freelance public relations specialist with a focus on crafting impactful PR campaigns for brands like [Company's Name]. Given your recent [product launch/expansion/news], I see an opportunity for a PR strategy that can further bolster your brand's image and reach. My recent campaign for [Previous Client or Project] achieved [specific results or coverage]. I'd be thrilled to share some tailored PR ideas for [Company's Name]. Could we set up a time to discuss this?

Best,
[Your Name]

Template 19: Freelance Content Marketer for Tech

Startups

Subject: Driving Engagement for [Start-up's Name] – Content Marketing Solutions

Hello [Client's Name],

As a freelance content marketer with a passion for the tech industry, I specialize in creating content that drives engagement and growth for startups like [Start-up's Name]. I've been impressed by your innovative approach and see great potential for content to further amplify your message. For [Previous Client/Project], I developed a content strategy that increased web traffic by [specific percentage]. I'd love to discuss how a comprehensive content plan could benefit your start-up. Can we schedule a chat?

Sincerely,
[Your Name]

Template 20: Freelance Translator Offering Language Services

Subject: Bridging Language Barriers – Professional Translation Services Available

Hi [Client's Name],

I am a professional freelance translator specializing in [languages]. I understand that [Company's Name] is expanding its reach in [specific markets or regions], and effective communication is key. My translation work has helped businesses like yours connect with a broader audience, maintaining the integrity and nuance of the original content. For instance, my translation for [Previous Client or Project] was instrumental in [specific outcome]. I'd be interested in discussing how my language services could support your expansion efforts.

Kind regards,
[Your Name]

Template 21: Freelance Mobile App Developer Offering Development Services

Subject: Enhance Your Digital Offering with Custom App Development

Hi [Client's Name],

As a freelance mobile app developer, I specialize in creating user-centric and innovative mobile applications. I've noticed [Company's Name]'s strong digital presence but observed an opportunity in the mobile app space. My recent project for [Previous Client/Project] resulted in an app that significantly improved user engagement and sales. I'd love to explore how a custom mobile app could benefit [Company's Name]. Can we discuss your digital strategy and how I can contribute?

Best regards,
[Your Name]

Template 22: Freelance SEO Content Writer

Targeting Niche Websites

Subject: Boosting [Niche/Industry] Content with SEO Best Practices

Dear [Client's Name],

I am a freelance writer with extensive experience in creating SEO-optimized content for [Niche/Industry]. Your website, [Website Name], is a fantastic resource in the [Niche/Industry] space, but I see the potential for even greater search engine visibility. My work with [Previous Client/Project] not only enhanced their online presence but also drove significant organic traffic. I'd like to share some ideas for content that could increase your website's visibility and engagement. Is this something you're interested in exploring?

Warm regards,
[Your Name]

Template 23: Freelance Graphic Designer for Branding Projects

Subject: Crafting Distinctive Brand Identities – Freelance Design Services

Hi [Client's Name],

As a creative freelance graphic designer, I have a passion for developing unique and impactful brand identities. I've been admiring [Company's Name]'s approach to branding and feel that my design style could complement and enhance your visual identity. My recent work for [Previous Client/Brand] involved creating a complete brand package that was highly acclaimed for its originality. I'd be excited to discuss how my design expertise can contribute to your branding efforts. Can we schedule a time to talk?

Best,
[Your Name]

Template 24: Freelance Digital Marketing Expert for Small Businesses

Subject: Scaling Your Business with Targeted Digital Marketing Strategies

Dear [Client's Name],

I specialize in digital marketing with a focus on helping small businesses grow their online presence. Having reviewed [Company's Name] and its digital marketing efforts, I believe there are untapped opportunities to increase your reach and customer engagement. My strategy for [Previous Client/Project] resulted in [specific results, like increased leads or sales]. I'd love to share how a targeted digital marketing strategy could yield similar results for your business. Are you available for a brief discussion?

Thank you,
[Your Name]

Template 25: Freelance Project Manager Offering Services to Startups

Subject: Streamlining Project Success for [Start-up's Name]

Hello [Client's Name],

I am a freelance project manager with a wealth of experience in steering projects to successful completion, particularly in startup environments. Your start-up, [Start-up's Name], has impressive potential, and effective project management can be key to harnessing it fully. I've led projects similar to [describe a relevant project] with [Previous Client/Project], achieving [specific outcomes or goals]. I'm interested in discussing how my project management skills could support and streamline your current and upcoming projects.

Sincerely,
[Your Name]

Template 26: Freelance Financial Consultant Offering Services to SMEs

Subject: Optimizing Financial Strategies for [Company's Name]

Hi [Client's Name],

As a freelance financial consultant with extensive experience working with SMEs, I specialize in optimizing financial strategies to enhance profitability and efficiency. I've observed [Company's Name]'s recent growth, and I believe there are opportunities to streamline your financial processes. My work with [Previous Client/Project] led to significant cost savings and revenue growth. Can we discuss how my expertise could support your financial goals?

Warm regards,
[Your Name]

Template 27: Freelance Interior Designer Reaching Out to Real Estate Firms

Subject: Transforming Spaces with Creative Interior Design

Dear [Client's Name],

I am a freelance interior designer passionate about creating functional and aesthetically pleasing spaces. Your real estate firm, [Firm's Name], has an impressive portfolio, and I see great potential for collaboration. My recent project for [Previous Client/Project] resulted in increased property value and client satisfaction. I'd love to share how my design solutions could enhance your properties. May I present some of my work for your consideration?

Best,
[Your Name]

Template 28: Freelance IT Consultant Offering Cybersecurity Solutions

Subject: Strengthening [Company's Name]'s Cybersecurity Posture

Hello [Client's Name],

In today's digital landscape, cybersecurity is crucial. As a freelance IT consultant specializing in cybersecurity, I help businesses safeguard their digital assets. I noticed [Company's Name] has been expanding its digital operations and believe there's an opportunity to enhance your cybersecurity measures. My work with [Previous Client/Project] led to robust security improvements and risk reduction. Can we schedule a call to discuss potential cybersecurity strategies for your company?

Thank you,
[Your Name]

Template 29: Freelance 3D Artist Offering Animation Services

Subject: Bringing Ideas to Life with 3D Animation

Hi [Client's Name],

I'm a freelance 3D artist with a talent for creating immersive and engaging animations. I've been following [Company's Name] and am excited about the kind of projects you undertake. My expertise in 3D animation could bring a new dimension to your work. For example, my recent animation for

[Previous Client/Project] was instrumental in their marketing campaign's success. I'd be happy to share some of my work that could align with your future projects.

Best regards,
[Your Name]

Template 30: Freelance E-learning Developer Reaching Out to Educational Institutions

Subject: Enhancing Learning Experiences with Custom E-learning Solutions

Dear [Client's Name],

As a freelance e-learning developer, I specialize in creating interactive and engaging online learning materials. I am impressed by [Institution's Name]'s commitment to innovative education methods and see a great opportunity for enhancing your e-learning content. My previous project for [Previous Client/Project] resulted in a notable increase in student engagement and learning outcomes. Could we discuss how my e-learning solutions could benefit your educational programs?

Warm regards,
[Your Name]

COLD MESSAGING TEMPLATES FOR SALES PITCHES

CHAPTER 75: SALES PITCHES: THE ART OF PERSUASION THROUGH COLD MESSAGING

Introduction

In sales, the initial message can make a significant difference. Cold messaging for sales pitches requires a blend of persuasion, clarity, and value proposition. This chapter focuses on crafting cold messages that not only capture the attention of potential clients but also persuade them to consider your product or service.

Understanding the Client's Needs

A successful sales pitch starts with understanding

the client's needs and challenges:

- Research the potential client's industry, company, and recent news or achievements.
- Identify how your product or service can solve a specific problem or enhance their operations.

Crafting a Compelling Value Proposition

Your cold message should clearly articulate the value proposition:

- Explain how your product or service stands out from competitors.
- Highlight the benefits and results that the client can expect.

Structuring Your Sales Pitch

An effective cold message for sales should include:

- An engaging subject line that piques curiosity.
- A brief introduction that establishes your credibility.
- A concise description of your offering and its unique value.
- A clear call to action, such as setting up a meeting or a product demonstration.

Building Rapport and Trust

Persuasion is not just about selling a product; it's about building a relationship:

- Show that you understand and care about the

client's business goals.

- Use a tone that is professional yet approachable.

Sample Cold Message Template for a Sales Pitch

Subject: Transform Your [Client's Industry] Operations with [Your Product/Service]

Hi [Client's Name],

I recently came across [Client's Company] and noticed that you're making significant strides in [specific area or project]. Our [Product/Service], with its proven track record in enhancing [specific benefit], seems like a perfect fit for your needs. For instance, [Your Product/Service] helped companies like [Example Company] achieve [specific results]. I'd be keen to explore how we could achieve similar results for [Client's Company]. Can we schedule a quick call to discuss this in detail?

Best regards,
[Your Name]

Conclusion

A well-crafted sales pitch cold message is your first step toward a successful sale. It should intrigue, inform, and invite the potential client to engage further. With the guidelines and template provided in this chapter, you're equipped to create persuasive cold messages that resonate with potential clients and set the stage for successful sales conversations.

CHAPTER 76-105: COLD MESSAGING TEMPLATES FOR SALES PITCHES

Template 1: Software Solution Sales Pitch

Subject: Streamline Your Workflow with [Software Solution Name]

Hi [Client's Name],

I understand that [Client's Company] is continually looking for ways to enhance productivity and streamline operations. Our software, [Software Solution Name], has been instrumental in helping similar businesses achieve these goals. It offers [mention key features and benefits]. Companies like [Example Company] have seen [specific improvements]. I'd love to arrange a demo to show how it could work for your team. When might be a convenient time for you?

Best regards,
[Your Name]

Template 2: B2B Service Offering

Subject: Elevating [Client's Company]'s [Service Area] to New Heights

Dear [Client's Name],

In today's competitive [industry] market, [specific service area] can be a game-changer. At [Your Company], we specialize in providing [specific service] that has helped businesses like yours achieve [specific results]. Our approach focuses on [key aspects of service]. I would appreciate the opportunity to discuss how we can bring these results to [Client's Company]. Can we schedule a call next week?

Warm regards,
[Your Name]

Template 3: Product Sales for Retail Businesses

Subject: Enhancing [Client's Company]'s Product Line with [Your Product]

Hello [Client's Name],

As [Your Position] at [Your Company], I've noticed that [Client's Company] is a leader in [industry/retail market]. Our product, [Your Product], aligns perfectly with your current offerings and has seen great success in similar stores. It stands out due to [mention unique selling points]. Retailers like [Example Retailer] experienced [mention specific benefits or sales increase]. Could we discuss how it might fit into your product lineup?

Thank you,
[Your Name]

Template 4: Consulting Services for Small Businesses

Subject: Unlocking Potential: Tailored Consulting for [Client's Company]

Hi [Client's Name],

Small businesses face unique challenges and opportunities, and our consulting services are designed to navigate these effectively. At [Your Company], we offer [specific consulting services] that have transformed businesses in [Client's Industry]. For example, we helped [Previous Client] to [specific achievement or improvement]. I believe a similar approach could benefit [Client's Company]. Would you be open to a brief meeting to explore this further?

Best,
[Your Name]

Template 5: Health and Wellness Product Pitch

Subject: Revolutionize Your Customers' Health and

Wellness with [Your Product]

Dear [Client's Name],

I've been following [Client's Company]'s focus on health and wellness, and it's impressive. Our product, [Your Product], aligns with your mission and has had remarkable success in enhancing [specific health/wellness benefit]. It's unique because [mention unique features or benefits]. Stores like [Example Store] saw [specific positive results]. I'd love to discuss how [Your Product] could be a valuable addition to your offerings. Is there a time next week that works for you?

Sincerely,
[Your Name]

Template 6: Eco-Friendly Product Sales to Retailers

Subject: Bringing Sustainable Choices to [Client's Company] with [Your Product]

Hi [Client's Name],

In a market increasingly driven by eco-conscious consumers, [Your Product] offers an excellent opportunity for [Client's Company] to expand its range of sustainable products. Our eco-friendly [product type] has been a hit with retailers focused on sustainability, helping them attract a growing demographic. Stores like [Example Store] have seen positive customer feedback and increased sales. Can we explore how [Your Product] can fit into your product lineup?

Best regards,
[Your Name]

Template 7: Corporate Training Program Offer

Subject: Empower Your Team with [Your Training Program]

Dear [Client's Name],

I specialize in corporate training programs that focus on [specific skill or area, e.g., leadership, communication]. I believe that [Your Training Program] could significantly benefit the team at [Client's Company] by [specific benefits]. For instance, our program at [Previous Client] led to marked improvements in [specific outcomes, e.g., team productivity]. I'd appreciate the opportunity to discuss tailoring our program to meet your team's needs. Are you available for a call next week?

Warm regards,
[Your Name]

Template 8: Innovative Tech Solution for B2B Clients

Subject: Transform Your Business Operations with [Your Tech Solution]

Hello [Client's Name],

As [Your Position] at [Your Company], I've

been closely following the challenges and trends in [Client's Industry]. Our solution, [Your Tech Solution], addresses common issues such as [specific problems] and has helped businesses streamline their operations. For example, our work with [Previous Client] resulted in [specific benefits or improvements]. I'd love to show you how [Your Tech Solution] could do the same for [Client's Company]. Can we arrange a demo at your convenience?

Thank you,
[Your Name]

Template 9: Specialty Food Product Introduction to Retailers

Subject: Introducing a Unique Culinary Experience with [Your Food Product]

Hi [Client's Name],

I represent [Your Company], creators of [Your Food Product], a unique addition to the culinary market. Our product has been well-received in markets similar to [Client's Company], offering a new and exciting choice for food enthusiasts. Retailers like [Example Retailer] have seen a significant uptick in customer interest and sales. I'd love to discuss how [Your Food Product] could be a great fit for your store. Would you be open to a tasting and discussion?

Best,
[Your Name]

Template 10: Custom Software Services for Small Businesses

Subject: Customized Software Solutions for [Client's Company]

Dear [Client's Name],

In an era where technology drives business success, our custom software services offer [Client's Company] the tools to stay ahead. We specialize in [specific types of software solutions], tailored to meet the unique needs of small businesses. Our clients, like [Previous Client], have experienced [specific improvements, e.g., increased efficiency, reduced costs]. I would like to discuss how our solutions can be customized for your specific business challenges. Are you available for a brief call to explore this?

Sincerely,
[Your Name]

Template 11: Professional Cleaning Services for Corporate Offices

Subject: Enhance Your Office Environment with [Your Cleaning Service]

Hi [Client's Name],

A clean and well-maintained office not only ensures a healthy workspace but also leaves a lasting impression on clients and employees.

At [Your Cleaning Service], we specialize in professional cleaning services tailored for corporate environments. Our work with companies like [Previous Client] has consistently resulted in improved workplace satisfaction and hygiene. I'd like to discuss how we can provide a customized cleaning solution for [Client's Company]. Can we arrange a meeting to explore this?

Best regards,
[Your Name]

Template 12: Specialized Printing Services for Marketing Campaigns

Subject: Elevate Your Marketing with High-Quality Printing Solutions from [Your Company]

Dear [Client's Name],

In the world of marketing, the quality of your printed materials can make a significant impact. [Your Company] offers specialized printing services that ensure your marketing campaigns stand out. We've helped businesses like [Previous Client] create eye-catching and memorable print materials. I believe [Client's Company] could greatly benefit from our expertise, especially for your upcoming [specific campaign or event]. Could we set up a time to discuss your printing needs?

Warm regards,
[Your Name]

Template 13: IT Support Services for Growing Businesses

Subject: Reliable IT Support for Seamless [Client's Company] Operations

Hello [Client's Name],

As [Client's Company] continues to grow, robust IT support becomes crucial. [Your Company] provides comprehensive IT support services that can adapt to your evolving business needs. Our clients, including [Previous Client], have experienced reduced downtime and enhanced IT efficiency. I'm confident that we can offer similar results for [Client's Company]. Would you be interested in learning more about our IT support solutions?

Thank you,
[Your Name]

Template 14: Creative Agency Services for Brand Development

Subject: Transforming [Client's Company]'s Brand Image with Creative Expertise

Hi [Client's Name],

A strong brand image is essential in today's competitive market, and [Your Creative Agency] is here to help you stand out. We specialize in holistic brand development, from visual identity to digital presence. Our recent project with [Previous

Client] led to a significant increase in their brand recognition and customer engagement. I'd love to share how our creative services could redefine [Client's Company]'s brand. Are you available for a brief discussion on this?

Best,
[Your Name]

Template 15: Custom Furniture Manufacturing for Hospitality Industry

Subject: Bespoke Furniture Solutions for [Client's Company]'s Unique Spaces

Dear [Client's Name],

In the hospitality industry, the ambiance is everything, and custom furniture plays a key role in creating unique and welcoming spaces. [Your Company] crafts high-quality, bespoke furniture that can enhance the aesthetic and functionality of spaces like those at [Client's Company]. Our collaboration with [Previous Client] in their recent renovation project received outstanding feedback. I'd be delighted to discuss how our custom solutions can meet your specific needs. Would you like to explore this further?

Sincerely,
[Your Name]

Template 16: Specialty Coffee Products for Cafés

Subject: Elevate [Café's Name]'s Coffee Experience with Our Specialty Blends

Hi [Client's Name],

As a lover of great coffee, I was drawn to [Café's Name] and its reputation for quality. Our company, [Your Company], specializes in sourcing and providing specialty coffee blends that can elevate any café's coffee experience. Our partnership with [Previous Client/Café] not only enhanced their coffee menu but also increased their customer satisfaction. I'd love to discuss how our unique blends could become a part of your offering. Would a coffee tasting session be possible?

Best regards,
[Your Name]

Template 17: Advanced Fitness Equipment for Gyms

Subject: Enhancing [Gym's Name] with Cutting-Edge Fitness Equipment

Dear [Client's Name],

In the fitness industry, the quality and variety of equipment can set a gym apart. [Your Company] offers the latest in advanced fitness equipment, designed to cater to a wide range of fitness enthusiasts. We've helped gyms like [Previous Client/Gym] upgrade their facilities, resulting in increased membership retention and satisfaction. Can we explore how our equipment range could fit into [Gym's Name]'s setup?

Warm regards,
[Your Name]

Template 18: Business Insurance Services for SMEs

Subject: Comprehensive Insurance Solutions for [Client's Company]'s Peace of Mind

Hello [Client's Name],

Protecting a business against unforeseen events is crucial, especially for growing SMEs like [Client's Company]. At [Your Insurance Company], we specialize in providing comprehensive business insurance solutions tailored to specific industry needs. Our clients, including [Previous Client], have found our personalized approach both reassuring and beneficial. I'd be happy to discuss how our insurance services can provide peace of mind and protection for your business. Are you available for a call next week?

Thank you,
[Your Name]

Template 19: HR Software Solutions for Efficient Workforce Management

Subject: Streamlining HR Processes at [Client's Company] with [Your Software Solution]

Hi [Client's Name],

Effective workforce management is key to any business's success. [Your Software Solution] offers innovative HR software that streamlines everything from payroll to employee engagement. Companies like [Previous Client] have seen remarkable improvements in HR efficiency and employee satisfaction. I believe [Client's Company] could greatly benefit from our software. Would you be open to a demo to see it in action?

Best,
[Your Name]

Template 20: Premium Catering Services for Corporate Events

Subject: Exceptional Catering for [Client's Company]'s Events

Dear [Client's Name],

For corporate events, the quality of catering can leave a lasting impression. At [Your Catering Service], we specialize in providing premium catering services that turn events into memorable experiences. Our attention to detail and commitment to quality have made events for clients like [Previous Client] stand out. I'd love the opportunity to discuss catering options for [Client's Company]'s upcoming events. Can we set up a meeting to go over your needs and preferences?

Sincerely,
[Your Name]

Template 21: Innovative SaaS Platform for Businesses

Subject: Transform [Client's Company]'s Operations with [Your SaaS Platform]

Hi [Client's Name],

In today's fast-paced business world, [Your SaaS Platform] can play a crucial role in enhancing operational efficiency and decision-making. We've helped businesses like [Previous Client] streamline their processes, resulting in [specific improvements, e.g., reduced costs, increased productivity]. I'm keen to show you how our platform can be customized to [Client's Company]'s specific needs. Would you be open to a demonstration?

Best regards,
[Your Name]

Template 22: Customized Packaging Solutions for Retailers

Subject: Stand Out on Shelves with Custom Packaging for [Client's Company]

Dear [Client's Name],

Eye-catching packaging can significantly impact product sales and brand perception. At [Your

Company], we provide customized packaging solutions that not only protect but also enhance product appeal. Our work with [Previous Client] led to an increase in shelf impact and customer engagement. I'd love to discuss how our packaging solutions could benefit [Client's Company]'s products. Can we arrange a meeting to explore this?

Warm regards,
[Your Name]

Template 23: Comprehensive Legal Services for Startups

Subject: Legal Support Tailored for [Client's Company]'s Startup Journey

Hello [Client's Name],

Navigating the legal landscape can be challenging for startups. Our firm, [Your Law Firm], specializes in comprehensive legal services tailored for the unique needs of startups like [Client's Company]. We've supported clients such as [Previous Client] in areas like [specific legal services, e.g., intellectual property, contracts]. I believe our expertise could be invaluable to your business. Would you be interested in a consultation to discuss your legal needs?

Thank you,
[Your Name]

Template 24: Advanced Analytics Services for E-

commerce

Subject: Boosting [Client's Company]'s E-commerce with Data-Driven Insights

Hi [Client's Name],

In e-commerce, leveraging data analytics can unlock new growth opportunities. [Your Company] offers advanced analytics services that can help you understand customer behavior and optimize your online store. For instance, our work with [Previous Client] resulted in [specific benefits, e.g., increased conversion rates]. I'd like to explore how our analytics expertise could drive similar results for [Client's Company]. Are you available for a discussion on this?

Best,
[Your Name]

Template 25: Exclusive Office Furniture Line for Modern Workspaces

Subject: Redefining [Client's Company]'s Workspace with [Your Furniture Line]

Dear [Client's Name],

A well-designed workspace can inspire creativity and enhance productivity. Our exclusive line of office furniture, [Your Furniture Line], offers both aesthetic appeal and ergonomic comfort. We've transformed spaces for clients like [Previous Client], creating environments that employees love. I'm eager to show you our range and discuss how it could fit into [Client's Company]'s office design. Could we schedule a time for you to view our collection?

Sincerely,
[Your Name]

Template 26: E-Learning Course for Professional Development

Subject: Empower Your Team with [Your E-Learning Course]

Hi [Client's Name],

In today's competitive environment, continuous learning is key. Our e-learning course, [Course Name], offers valuable skills in [specific subject or skill]. It's been a game-changer for companies like [Previous Client], where teams enhanced their capabilities and productivity. I'd love to discuss how [Client's Company] could benefit from our courses. Is there a good time for a quick call to explore this?

Best regards,
[Your Name]

Template 27: Digital Marketing E-Book for Small Business Owners

Subject: Grow Your Business with Insights from Our Digital Marketing E-Book

Dear [Client's Name],

As a small business owner, staying ahead in digital marketing is crucial. Our e-book, [E-Book Title], provides actionable insights and strategies tailored for small businesses. It has helped entrepreneurs like those at [Previous Client/Company] significantly improve their online presence. I think it could be a great resource for [Client's Company]. Would you be interested in a free sample chapter?

Warm regards,
[Your Name]

Template 28: Subscription-Based Design Tool for Freelancers

Subject: Enhance Your Design Work with [Your Design Tool]

Hello [Client's Name],

For freelancers, having the right tools is essential for success. [Your Design Tool] is a subscription-based tool that offers [key features, e.g., templates, customization options]. It's been instrumental for freelancers like [Previous Client/User], enabling them to create stunning designs efficiently. I'd like to offer you a free trial to see how it can streamline your workflow. Are you interested in giving it a try?

Thank you,

[Your Name]

Template 29: Online Fitness Program for Health Enthusiasts

Subject: Achieve Your Fitness Goals with [Your Online Program]

Hi [Client's Name],

Staying fit and healthy has never been more important. Our online fitness program, [Program Name], provides comprehensive workout and nutrition plans that you can follow from home. Users like [Previous Client/User] have seen remarkable results. I believe [Client's Company]'s focus on health and wellness makes it a perfect match for our program. Can we arrange a demo session for you to experience it firsthand?

Best,
[Your Name]

Template 30: Cloud-Based Accounting Software for Startups

Subject: Streamlining Finances with [Your Accounting Software]

Dear [Client's Name],

Managing finances efficiently is vital for any startup. [Your Accounting Software] is a cloud-based solution designed to simplify and automate accounting tasks. It's been a valuable tool for startups like [Previous Client/Company], helping them manage their finances with greater ease and accuracy. I'd be happy to show you how it can do the same for [Client's Company]. Would you be open to a walkthrough of our software?

Sincerely,
[Your Name]

CONCLUSION

EMPOWERING YOUR COLD MESSAGING JOURNEY

Reflecting on the Journey

As we reach the conclusion of "Cold Message Mastery," it's important to reflect on the journey we've embarked upon together. From understanding the nuances of cold messaging in different professional contexts to exploring over 100 tailored templates, this book has been a comprehensive guide to mastering the art of cold outreach.

Key Takeaways

- **Personalization is Key:** The success of a cold message largely depends on how well it is personalized and tailored to the recipient's needs and interests.
- **Clarity and Conciseness:** Effective cold

messages are clear, concise, and to the point, respecting the recipient's time and attention.

- **Building Relationships:** Cold messaging is not just about immediate gains but about building long-term professional relationships.
- **Adaptability:** The provided templates are starting points. Adapt them to suit your unique voice, style, and the specific requirements of each situation.

The Power of Persistence

Remember, cold messaging is a numbers game, and persistence is crucial. Not every message will receive a response, but each message is a step forward in honing your skills and expanding your network or client base.

Continual Learning and Adaptation

The landscape of professional communication is ever-evolving. Stay adaptable, keep learning, and evolve your cold messaging strategies to align with current trends and best practices.

Encouragement for the Road Ahead

As you apply the insights and templates from this book, remember that each message you send is a reflection of your professionalism and ambition. Whether you are seeking a job, an internship, freelance opportunities, or making a sales pitch, your dedication and skill in crafting effective cold messages can open doors to countless opportunities.

Final Words

"Cold Message Mastery" has equipped you with the tools and knowledge to make a mark in your professional endeavors. As you move forward, carry the lessons learned and remember that the art of cold messaging, much like any skill, improves with practice and perseverance.

LOOKING AHEAD – THE FUTURE OF COLD MESSAGING

Embracing the Future of Professional Communication

As we close this comprehensive guide on cold messaging, it's important to look towards the future and anticipate how the landscape of professional communication might evolve. Cold messaging, while rooted in timeless principles of communication, will continue to adapt to new technologies and shifting professional norms.

Anticipating Technological Advances

- **AI and Personalization:** Emerging technologies like AI are poised to offer even more sophisticated levels of personalization in messaging.
- **Virtual and Augmented Reality:** As these technologies become more mainstream, they could offer new platforms for innovative cold

messaging experiences.

Adapting to Changing Professional Landscapes

- **Globalization:** As the professional world becomes more interconnected, cold messaging will play a crucial role in crossing geographical and cultural barriers.
- **Remote Work and Digital Nomadism:** These trends will influence how professionals network and connect, possibly leading to more diverse and widespread cold messaging strategies.

Staying Ahead of the Curve

- **Continuous Learning:** Stay informed about the latest trends and technologies in communication and networking.
- **Experimentation:** Don't be afraid to try new platforms or approaches to cold messaging as the professional world evolves.

The Ongoing Journey

- **A Lifelong Skill:** Mastering cold messaging is not a one-time achievement but a continuous journey of learning, adapting, and refining your skills.
- **Building Your Network:** Continue to use cold messaging to expand your professional network, explore new opportunities, and build lasting relationships.

Final Encouragement

As you move forward in your professional journey, remember that the skills and insights gained from this book are just the beginning. Continue to hone your approach, adapt to new environments, and embrace the ever-changing landscape of professional communication. The future of cold messaging is an exciting frontier, and you are now well-equipped to navigate it successfully.